Thomas Bennett

A Selection of Phrases for Tourists Travelling in Norway

Thomas Bennett

A Selection of Phrases for Tourists Travelling in Norway

ISBN/EAN: 9783743340473

Manufactured in Europe, USA, Canada, Australia, Japa

Cover: Foto ©Lupo / pixelio.de

Manufactured and distributed by brebook publishing software
(www.brebook.com)

Thomas Bennett

A Selection of Phrases for Tourists Travelling in Norway

A

ECTION OF PHRAS

FOR

TOURISTS TRAVELLING IN NORWAY.

BY

T. BENNETT.

CHRISTIANIA. — B. M. BENTZEN.

1870.

The h after a vowel signifies that the latter is to be pronounced long; for instance, ohg like the interjection oh with a hard g at the end; thus, ohg has the sound of ogue in *rogue*; ehr like the interjection eh with r at the end; thus, ehr has the sound of *air*, pronounced quickly; ahm like the interjection ah with m at the end; thus, ahm has the sound of *alm* in *calm*; when, however, ah is followed by a double consonant, it has not the prolonged interjectional sound, but is pronounced like a in *father*; uh like ooh in the interjection *pooh*. The ä has the sound of a in *manna, senna, hookah;* y when it does not commence a syllable or come after an apostrophe, is pronounced like the French u, and ø like the French eu: in some of the phrases this is stated in a parenthetical remark; in others it has been omitted. The Norwegian g is *always* pronounced hard.

☞ *Should any useful sentences, not found in this book, occur to the traveller, it is requested that he will insert them in the blank leaves at the end, and give or forward them to the editor.*

English.	Norwegian.	Pronunciation.
Account.	See Bill.	
Ale.	See Beer.	
Apron.	Clean the apron of my car- riole.	Reengjør Skvætlæderet af min Kariol.	Rehn-yurr sqvetlehr-utt ah' min Kahrr-ee-ohl.
Axle, Axle- tree.	Will you get this axle — ax- letree mended.	Vil De faa denne Hjulaxel istandsat.	Vil Dee foh dennä Yuhl-axel ee-stalnnsahtt.
Bacon.	I should like some bacon and eggs.	Kan jeg faa Flesk og Æg?	Kahnn yei foh Flesk ohg Egg?
Bale.	Have you any thing to bale out the boat with?	Har De Noget at øse Baa- den lens?	Hahr de nohg-utt ahtt øsa Bohd-unn lenns?
Basin.	See Washhand Basin.		
Bathe.	Is there a place where I can bathe?	Findes der et Sted hvor jeg kan bade?	Finn-uss dehr et Stehd vohr yei kahnn bahdä?
Bear.	Are there any bears in this neighbourhood?	Findes der Bjørne i Omeg- nen?	Finn-uss dehr B'yurrnä ee Omm-ein-unn?
Bed.	Can I have a bed?	Kan jeg faa Seng?	Kahnn yei foh Seng.
Bed.	Let me see my bed.	Kan jeg faa se min Seng?	Kahnn yei foh sehninn Seng?
Bedroom.	Where is my bedroom?	Hvor er mit Sovekammer?	Vohr ehr mitt Sovä-kahmmer?
Beef, beef- steak.	Can I have roast beef — a beefsteak for breakfast — dinner — supper?	Kan jeg faa Oxesteg — Boeuf til Frokost — Middag — til Aftens.	Kahnn yei foh Oxä-stehg — Biff till Froh-kost — Mid- dahg — Ahfftunns?

1*

	English	Danish	Pronunciation
Beer.	Have you any beer?	Har De Øl?	Hahrr Dee Øl?
	Bring another bottle of beer.	Skaf mig en Flaske Øl til.	Skahff mig en Flahsskå Øl till.
Bill.	Bring me my bill.	Lad mig faa min Regning.	Lahd mei foh min Reining.
	The bill is very dear.	Regningen er meget høi.	Reining-unn ehr mehg-utt hø-ei.
Biscuit.	Have you any biscuits?	Kan jeg faa nogle Kjex?	Kahnn yei foh nohg-lä K'yex?
Blackgame.	Are there any blackgame in this neighbourhood?	Findes der Urfugl her i Nærheden (Blackcock = Urhan, pron. Uhrhahnn; Grayhen = Urhøne, pron. Uhrhønä).	Finn-uss dehr Uhrfuhl hehr ee Nehr-heddun?
Blacksmith.	Is there a blacksmith near here?	Boer der en Smed i Nærheden?	Boh-urr dehr en Smehi Nehr-heddunn?
Blanket.	I should like blankets instead of a featherbed.	Jeg vilde gjerne have et Uldtæppe istedenfor Dynen.	Yei vil-dä yehrnä hahvä et Oolteppä (ool as in wool) ee-stehd-enfohr Dyn-unn (y like the French u).
Boat.	I want a boat to take me to —	Jeg ønsker Baadskyds til —	Yei ønsk-urr Bohd-schyss till —
	Let the boat be ready by — o'clock.	Baaden maa være færdig Klokken —	Bohd-unn moh vehrä fehrdigg Klokkunn —
Boots.	Please to clean — grease my shoes — boots.	Vær saa god at pudse—smøre mine Skoe — Støvler.	Vehr soh goh aht puss-ä — snurrä meenä Sko — Stuvvlurr.
	Do not put my boots near the fire.	Sæt ikke mine Støvler nær Ilden.	
	Can you get these shoes — boots heeled — soled — mended?	KanDe faa disse Skoe—Støvler flikkede — saalede — lappede.	Kahnn Dee foh dizzä Sko — Stuvvlurr flikkädä — sohlädä — lappädä.
	Where is the boy to show us the way?	Hvor er den Dreng, der skal vise os Veien?	Vohr ehr den Dreng, dehr skahll veesä os Vei-unn?

Boy.	Where is the boy that is to go with me?	Hvor er Skydsgutten?	Vohr ehr Schyss-goottunn ? (oo as in crook).
Brandy.	Bring me a glass of brandy.	Lad mig faa et Glas Cognac.	Lah mei foh et Glahss Kohn-y'ac.
Bread.	Let me have a glass of hot brandy and water.	Kan jeg faa et Glas Toddy?	Kahnn yei foh et Glahss Tod-dy?
	Have you wheaten bread — rusks ?	Har De Franskbrød — Kav- ringer?	Hahr Dee Fransk-brød — kahv-ring-urr?
	This bread is too stale.	Dette Brød er for gammelt.	Dettä Brød ehr fohr gahmn-ult.
Breakfast.	Bring me some bread and butter.	Bring mig Brød og Smør (Smørrebrød means slices of bread and butter).	Bring mei Brød ohg Smurr (Smurräbrød).
	What can I have for break- fast?	Hvad kan jeg faa til Fro- kost?	Vah kahnn yei foh till Froh- kost ?
	I wish to have breakfast at — o'clock.	Jeg vil gjerne spise til Fro- kost Klokken —	Yei vill yehrnä speesä till Frohkost Klokkun.
Bridle.	Have you a bridle?	Har De en Bidsel?	Hahr Dee en Biss-ull?
Broth.	Can I have a little broth?	Kan jeg faa lidt klar Kjød- suppe?	Kahnn yei foh litt klahrr K'yød–sooppä?
Buckle.	Will you fasten a buckle here.	Vær saa snild at gjøre Spæn- den fast.	Vehr soh snill ahtt yørä Spenn-unn fahsst.
Butter.	Bring in some fresh butter.	Skaf mig lidt ferskt Smør.	Skahff mei litt fehrskt Smurr.
Button.	Will you sew a button on —	Vil De sy en Knap paa —	Vill De sy (y like the French u) en Knählpp poh.
Cab.	Fetch me a cab.	Hent mig en Droske — Hy- revogn.	Hent mei en Droschä — Hy- råvoggn.

Call.	Call me at — o'clock in the morning.	Væk mig imorgen Klokken —	Vekk mei ee-morg-unn Klok-kunn —
Candle.	Will you bring me a candle.	Vil De skaffe mig et Lys.	Vill Dee skaffa mei et Lys (y like the French u).
Capercaille	I had no candles.	Jeg fik ingen Lys.	Jei fik ing-unn Lyss.
	Are there any capercaillie in this part?	Findes der Tiur. The cock bird, Tiur, pron. Teeuhr; the hen, Røie, pron. Rei-å.	Finn-uss dehr Tee-uhr.
Carpet-bag	Strap my carpet-bag on the carriole.	Bind min Vadsæk fast paa Kariolen.	Binnd minn Vah-sekk fahsst poh Kahrr-ee-ohl-unn.
Carriage.	See Carriole.	Carriage = Vogn (pr. Voggn). An open 4 wheeled carriage = Trille (pr. Trillä).	
Carriole.	Will you wash my carriole — grease the wheels of my carriole.	Vil De vaske min Kariol — smøre Hjulene af min Kariol.	Vill Dee vahss-kämimnKahrr-ee-ohl — smurrä Yuhl-änä ah' minn Kahrr-ee-ohl.
Cart.	I want a cart for my luggage.	Jeg behøver en Kjærre for mit Tøi.	Yei bä-høvurr en K'yerrä fohr mit Tøi. (See Tarpauling.)
	Have you a cart with springs?	Har De en Kjærre med Fjær?	Hahrr Dee en K'yerrä meh F'ychr?
Cartridge.	Where can I buy some cartridges?	Hvor kan jeg faa kjøbt nogle Patroner?	Vohr kahnn yei foh k'yøbt nohg-lä Pah-trohn-urr?
Chamberpot	Will you bring a chamberpot.	De har glemt Natpotten.	Dee hahrr glemnt Naht-pottunn.
Change.	Have you any change?	Har De nogle Smaapenge?	Hahrr Dee nolg-lä Smoh-pengä? (ng as in ring).
Cheese.	Have you any English—Swiss — Dutch cheese?	Har De engelsk — sveitser — hollandsk Ost?	Hahrr Dee eng-ulsk, sveilz-urr — hollahnnsk Ohst?

English	Danish	Pronunciation
Where is the nearest chemist's shop?	Hvor er det nærmeste Apothek?	Vohr ehr dä nehrrus-tä Ah-pohtehk?
Have you any mutton — lamb chops?	Kan jeg faa nogle Faare — Lamme-Coteletter?	Kahnn yei foh nohg-lä Fohrä — Lahmmä-Kotlä-tetturr?
Where is the church?	Hvor ligger Kirken?	Vohr ligg-urr Keerk-unn?
How far off is the church?	Hvor langt er det til Kirken?	Vohr lahnngt ehr deh till keerk-unn?
What time does the service begin?	Hvad Tid begynder Gudstjenesten?	Vah Teed bägynnurr Guhds-t'ychnä-stunn?
Have you any claret — champagne — hock?	Har De Rødviin — Champagne — Rhinskviin?	Hahr Dee Rødveen (ø like the French u) — Shahmm-pahmiä — Rhinnsk-veen?
Where is the clergyman's house?	Hvor ligger Præstegaarden?	Vohr ligg-urr Prestä-gohrd-unn?
How far off is the clergyman's house?	Hvor langt er det til Præstegaarden?	Vohr lahnngt ehr deh till Prestä-gohrd-unn?
I should like a roast — boiled chicken for breakfast — dinner — super.	Kan jeg faa en stegt — kogt Kyling til Frokost — til Middag — til Aftens.	Kahnn yei foh en stehgt — kohgt K'ylling (y like the French u) till Frohkost — till Middahg — till Ahfftunns?
Call me at — o'clock, a quarter past six, half-past six, a quarter to seven.	Væk mig Klokken — et Kvarter over sex, halv syv, tre Kvarter i syv.	Vekk mei Klok-kunn — et et K'vahrr-tehr o-vurr sex, hahllv syv, treh K'vahrr-tehr ee syv.
Let me have a clothes-brush.	Skaf mig en Kladebørste.	Skahff mei en Klehdä-burrstä.
Please to brush my coat.	Vær saa snild at børste min Frakke.	Vehr soh snill aht burrstä minn Frahkkä.

English	Danish	Pronunciation
Will you make me some coffee.	Vil De koge mig lidt Kaffe.	Vill Dee kohg-ä mei litt Kahflä.
Bring in some cream.	Lad mig faa lidt Fløde.	Lah mei foh litt Flødä (the ø like the French eu).
Bring in a cup — cups.	Skaf mig en Kop — Kopper.	Skahff mei en Kopp — Kop-purr.
Have you any veal cutlets?	Kan jeg faa nogle Kalve-Coleleter?	Kahnn yei foh nohg-lä Kahlvä Koltä-letturr?
Bring me the daybook.	Bring mig Dagbogen.	Bring mei Dahg-bohg-unn.
What can I have for dinner?	Hvad kan jeg faa til Mid-dag?	Vah kahnn yei foh till Mid-dahg?
I should like to dine at — o'clock.	Jeg vil gjerne spise til Mid-dag Klokken —	Yei vill yehrnä speesä till Middahg Klokkunn —
Where does the doctor live?	Hvor boer Lægen?	Vohr boh-urr Legh-unn?
Give my dog something to eat.	Lad Hunden faa Noget at spise.	Lah lloon-unn (oo as in hood foh nohg-utt ahtt speesä.
What can I have to drink?	Hvad kan jeg faa at drikke?	Vah kahnn yei foh att drikkä?
Drive faster — slower.	Kjør hurtigere — sagtere.	K'yurr hoortigg-urrä—sahgt-urrä.
Dry my things — clothes.	Tør mit Tøi — mine Klæder.	Tør mitt Tø-ei — meenä Kleh-urr.
Are there any wild ducks in this neighbourhood?	Findes der vilde Ænder her i Nærheden?	Finn-uss dehr villä Enn-urr hehr ee Nehr-heddunn?
What can I have to eat?	Hvad kan jeg faa at spise?	Vah kahnn yei foh aht speesä?

Eggs.	I should like some boiled eggs — poached eggs.	Kan jeg faa blødkogte Æg — Speilæg?	Kahnn yei foh blødkohgtä (ø like the French eu) Egg — Speil-egg?
Eider-duck	Are there eider-ducks in the neighbourhood?	Findes der Ederfugl her i Narheden?	Finn-uss dehr Eddurrfuhl hehr ee Nehr-heddunn?
Elk.	Are there elks in this forest?	Findes der Elsdyr i denne Skov?	Finn-uss dehr Elssdyr (y like the French u) ee dennä Skohv?
Enough.	That is enough.	Det er nok.	Deh ehr nokk.
Far. Felloe— Felly.	How far is it to? Can you put a new felloe to this wheel?	Hvor langt er det til? Kan De skaffe en ny Fælge til dette Hjuul?	Vohr lahnngt ehr deh till? Kahnn Dee skahffä en ny (y like the French u) Feh-lä till dennä Yuhl?
Fire.	I should like a fire in the stove.	Vær saa god at lægge i Ovnen.	Vehr soh goh ahtf leggä ee Ov-nunn.
Fish.	Are there many fish in this river — lake? Will you boil — fry this fish.	Er der mange Fisk i denne Elv — dette Vand? Vil De koge — stege Fisken.	Ehr dehr mahng-ä Fisk ee dennä Elv — dettä Vahnn? Vill Dee kohg-ä — stehg-ä Fisk-unn.
Fishing—rod.	Where can I lay my fishing-rod?	Hvor kan jeg lægge min Fiskestang.	Vohr kahnn yei leg-gä min Fiskä-stahnng?
Fork.	See Knife.		
Fowls.	See Chickens.		
Frying-pan	Have you a frying-pan?	Har De en Stegepande?	Hahrr Dee en Stehgä-pahnnä?
Fusees.	See Matches.		
Game.	Have you any game in the house?	Har De noget Vildt?	Hahrr Dee nohg-utt Villt?

English	Norwegian	Pronunciation
Gin,	Let me have a bottle of gin*).	Lad mig faa en Flaske Aqvavit.	Lah mei foh enn Flahsskä Akkävilt.
Girth.	Buckle the girths a little tighter.	Spænd Sadelgjordene lidt strammere.	Spenn Sahll-yohr-unnä litt strahmm-urrä.
Glass.	Bring me a glass — wineglass — tumbler.	Bring mig et Glas — Viinglas — Ølglas.	Bring mei et Glahss -- Veen-glahss — Ølglahss (the ø like the French eu).
Grease.	Grease the weels of my carriole — carriage.	Smör Kariol — Vogn-Hjulene.	Smurr Kahrr-ee-ohl — Voggn-Yuhl-änä.
Grocer.			
Grouse.	Have you any grease? See Shop. Are there any grouse near here?	Har De Smørelse? Findes der Tiur — Urfugl — Hjerper — Ryper i Omegnen?	Hahrr De Smurr-uläs? Finn-uss dehr Tee-uhr—Uhr-fool — Yehrpurr — Ryp-urr (the y like the French u) ee Om-ein-unn?
Guide.	I want a guide to show me the way to —.	Jeg ønsker en Fører for at vise mig Veien til —.	Jei ønsk-urr en Før-urr fohr ahtt veesa mei Vei-unn till —.
Gun.	Can you clean a gun?	Kan De reengjøre et Gevær en Bøsse?	Kahnn Dee rehn-yørä et Gávehr (g hard as in gel) en Bøssä (ø like the French eu).
Gunpowder	Where can I buy gunpowder?	Hvor kan jeg faa kjøbt noget Krudt?	Vohr kahnn yei foh k'yøpt (the ø like the French eu) nohg-utt Kroodt?
Hammer.	Bring a hammer and nails?	Lad mig faa en Hammer og Spiger.	Lah mei foh en Hahnnn-urr ohg Speeg-urr.

*) No spirits are allowed to be sold in the country except at the „stores". „Throndhjemsk" (pron. trønn-yemsk). English gin is not to be had.

The best „aquavit" is called

Hare.	Are there any hares near here?	Findes der Harer her i Nær- heden?	Finn-uss dehr Hahr-urr hehr i Nehr-heddun?
Harness.	Get this harness repaired?	Faa Sælen istandsat.	Foh Setl-unn ee-stahnnsatt.
Haste.	Make haste.	Skynd dig.	Shynn dei!
Hazelhen.	Are there any hazelhens in the wood?	Findes der Hjerper i Skoven?	Finn-uss dehr Yehrpurr ee Skov-unn?
Horse.	Let me have a horse without harness — with harness — with saddle and bridle to as soon as possible — immediately.	Lad mig faa en løs Hest — en Hest med Sæle — med Sadel og Bidsel til — saa snart som muligt — strax.	Lah mei foh en løs (the ø like the French eu) Hest en Hest meh Sehlä — med Sahl ohg Bissul — till — soh snahrt som muhligt — strax.
Hour.	How many hours? Let me have — in a quarter of an hour — in three quarters of an hour.	Hvor mange Timer? Lad mig faa — om et Kvar- ter — om en halv Time — om tre Kvarter.	Kahnn duh ikkä k'yørä toh Shift-urr? Vohr mangä Teem-urr? Lah mei foh — om et Kvahrr- tehr — om en hahll Teem-ä — om treh Kvahrr-tehr.
Ink.	Bring me a pen and ink.	Skaf mig Pen og Black.	Skahff mei Pen ohg Blek.
Knife.	Bring me a knife and fork.	Lad mig faa Kniv og Gaffel.	Lah mei foh K'neev ohg Gahff-ull.
Lamb.	Have you any lamb?	Har De Lammekjød?	Hahrr Dee Lahmmä-k'yöd?
Landing- net.	Please to give me my land- ing-net.	Vær saa snil at give mig min Fiske-Hov.	Vehr soh snill ahtt geevä mei min Fiskhä-Hohv.
Left.	To the left?	Til Venstre!	Till Venn-strä?
Lemon.	Have you a lemon?	Har De en Citron?	Hahrr Dee en Sit-trohn?
Lobster.	Have you any lobsters?	Har De Hummer?	Hahrr Dee Hoomm-urr (oo as in book)?

English	Danish	Pronunciation
Look alive!	Skynd dig! Vær lidt snart!	Shynn dei! Vehr lidt snahrt!
See Matches.		
Let me have sume luncheon.	Lad mig faa Noget at spise.	Lah mei foh Nohg-utt ahtt speesä.
Will you give me some matches.	Lad mig faa nogle Fyrstikker.	Lah mei foh nohg-lä Fyr- stik-kurr.
Have you a mattrass instead of this feather-bed?	Har De en Madrasse istedel- for Underdynen?	Hahrr Dee en Mah-drahssä ce- stehdutlfor Oon-durr-dy- nunn (o as in book, y like the French u).
Have you any fresh meat in the house.	Har De noget ferskt Kjød?	Hahr Dee nohg-utl fehrskt K'yød (the ø like the French eu).
Lat me have a glass — cup — basin of milk — a bowl of curded milk with the cream on it	Lad mig faa et Glass — en Kop — en Bolle Melk — en Ringe (Kolle) Fløde- melk.	Lah mei foh et Glahss — en Kopp — en Bolli Melk — en Ring-ä (Kolla) Flø- dä-melk (ø like the French eu).
Let me have — in — minutes.	Lad mig faa — om — Mi- nutter.	Lah mei foh — om — Min-oot- urr (oo as in crook).
How much?	Hvor meget?	Vohr mehg-utt?
Bring some mustard.	Bring lidt Sennep.	Bring litt Senn-ep.
Can I have roast mutton — a mutton chop for breakfast — dinner — supper?	Kan jeg faa Faaresteg — en Faare-Cotelet til Fro- kost — Middag — Aftens?	Kahnn yei foh Fohr-ä-stehg — en Fohrä--kottälet till Frohkost — Middahg — Ahfftunns?
See Hammer.		
What is the name of this that place.	Hvad hedder dette — hint Sted?	Vah hed-durr dettä — hvent Stehd?

Needle.	Bring me a needle and black — white thread.	Lad mig faa Naal og sort — hvid Traad.	Lah mei foh Nohl ohg sohrt — veed Troh.
Oil.	Bring a little oil for my gun.	Bring lidt Olie for mit Gevær — min Bøsse.	Bring litt Ohleeä fohr mitt Gä-vehr — minn Bøssä.
Omelet.	Can you make an omelet.	Kan De lave en Omelet (Æggekage)?	Kahnn Dee lahvä en Omm'lett (Eggä-kahgg-ä)?
Onion.	Fry some onions with the meat.	Lad mig faa Løg til Kjødet.	Lah mei foh Løg (ø like the French eu) til K'yöd-utt.
Oysters.	Are there any oysters to be had?	Er der Østers at faa?	Ehr dehr Østurrs ahtt foh?
Pancake.	Can you make some pancakes?	Kan De lave nogle Pandekager?	Kahnn Dee lahvä nohg-lä Pahnn-ä-kahg-ä?
Pay.	What have I to pay?	Hvad har jeg at betale?	Vah hahrr yei ahtt bä-tahlä?
	What do I owe?	Hvad skylder jeg?	Vah schyllurr yei?
Pen.	See Ink.		
Pepper.	Bring some pepper.	Bring lidt Pebber.	Bring litt Pehb-urr.
Percussion cap.	Where can I buy percussion caps?	Hvor kan jeg faa kjøbt Knalhætter?	Vohr kahnn yei foh k'yøbt (the ø like the French eu) k'nahll-hetturr?
Physician.	See Doctor.		
Pillow-case.	Let me have a clean pillow-case.	Lad mig faa et reent Pudevaar — Pudebetræk.	Lah mei foh en rehn Puhdä-vahr-ä — Puhdä-bä-trekk.
Pincers.	Have you a pair of pincers?	Har De en Knibtang?	Hahrr Dee en K'neebtahnng? (the ng as in ring).
Plate.	Bring a clean plate — clean plates.	Bring en reen Tallerken — rene Tallerkener.	Bring en rehn Tahll-ehrkunn — rehnä Tahll-ehrkunnur.
Please.	Please to —	Vær saa snild at —	Vehr soh snill ahtt —
Porter.	Have you any English porter?	Har De engelsk Porter?	Hahrr Dee engelsk Porter?

Portman-teau.	Bring in my portmanteau.	Bring ind Kufferten.	Bring inn Kooffurt-unn (the oo in Kooffurt-unn like oo in cook).
	Put my portmanteau on the carriole.	Bind min Kuffert fast paa Kariolen.	Binnd minn Kooffurt (see the preceding) fahsst poh Kahrr-ee-ohl-unn.
Posting-station.	Where is the posting-station?	Hvor er Skydsskiftet?	Vohr ehr Shys-shift-utt?
Post-office.	Take this letter to the post-office.	Bring dette Brev paa Post-huset (in the country called Postaabneriet).	Bring dett Brehv poh Posst-konn-tohr-utt — Possl-huhs-utt.
	Where is the post-office?	Hvor er Posthuset?	Vohr ehr Posst-huhs-utt — Posst-konn-tohr-utt?
Potatoes.	Let me have potatoes with —	Lad mig faa Poteter til —	Lah mei foh Poh-tehturr til —
Price.	What is the price of this-that?	Hvad koster dette — det?	Vahd kost-urr dettä — deh?
Privy.	Will you show me the way to the privy.	Hvor er Locumet — Priv-tet — Vandhuset — Das?*)	Vohr ehr Locum-utt — Priv-eht-utt — Vahnn-huhss-utt — Dahss?
Ptarmigan.	Are there any ptarmigan about here?	Findes der Ryper i Omeg-nen?	Finn-uss dehr Rypurr (the y like the French u) ee Omm-ein-unn?
Pudding.	Can I have any pudding?	Kan jeg faa Budding?	Kahn yei foh Bood-ding (oo as in book).
Quick.	Be quick!	Vær snar!	Vehr snahrr!
Raspberries	Have you any raspberries?	Har De Bringebær?	Hahrr De Bring-ähehr?

Ready.	Are the horses ready?	Ere Hestene færdige?	Ehrä Hest-unni fehr-diggï?
Reindeer.	Are there any reindeer on the mountains?	Er der Rensdyr — Reen paa Fjeldet?	Ehr dehr Rennsdyr (y like the French u) — Rehn poh Fyel-utt?
Right.	To the right?	Til Høire?	Till Hø-ei-ra Hø-ei pron. in one syllable)?
River.	Is there a river near here?	Er der nogen Elv i Nær-heden?	Ehr dehr nohg-unn Elv ee Nehr-heddunn?
Road.	Which is the road to —?	Hvilken er Veien til —?	Vilkunn ehr Vei-unn til —?
Saddle-horse.	I want a saddle-horse.	Jeg ønsker Hest med Sadel.	Jei ønsk-urr Hest meh Sahll.
Salmon.	Is there any salmon-fishing to be had near here?	Er der Anledning til at fiske Lax nogetsteds i Omeg-nen?	Ehr dehr Ahnn-lehd-ning ahtt fiskï Lahx nohg-ull-stehds ee Omm-ein-unn?
Salt.	You have forgotten the salt.	De har glemt at bringe Salt.	Dee hahr glemmt ahtt bring-ä Sahlt.
Servant.	Tell the servant to come. Waiter!	Bed Pigen (maid-servant) Tjeneren (man-servant) komme hid. Opvarter!	Beh Peeg-unn, T'ychnurr-unn kommï heed. Op-vahrr-turr!
Shaft.	Can you mend this shaft?	Kan De istandsætte denne Kariolarm?	Kahnn Dee ee-stahnn-settï dennï Kahrr ee-ohl-ahrm?
Sheets.	Put clean sheets on the bed.	Lad mig faa rene Lagener.	Lah mei foh rehnï Lahg-unn-urr.
Sherry.	Let me have a glass — bottle of sherry.	Lad mig faa et Glas — en Flaske Sherry.	Lah mei foh et Glahss — en Flahss-kï Sherry.
Shirt.	Will you get this shirt washed.	Vær saa snild at faa denne Skjorte vasket.	Vehr soh snill ahtt foh dennï Shohrtï vahss-kutt.
	How long before it will be ready?	Naar kan den blive færdig?	Nohr kahnn den bleevï fehr-diggï?

English	Danish	Pronunciation
Shoemaker} Shoes	See Boots.	
Shop (in the country).	Is there any shop near here?	Boer der nogen Landhandler i Nærheden?	Boh-urr dehr nohg-unn Lahn-hahnd-lurr ee Nehr-hed-dunn?
Smith.	See Blacksmith.	
Snipes.	Are there any snipes in the neighbourhood?	Findes der Snepper i Om-egnen?	Finn-uss dehr Sneppurr ee Omm-ein-unn?
Soap.	Bring some soap.	Bring mig et Stykke Sæbe.	Bring mei et Stykkă Schbă.
Soup.	Please to warm this soup.	Vær saa snild at varme Sup-pen.	Vehr soh snill aht vahrna Sooppunn (oo in Sooppunn as in crook).
Spoke.	Can you put a new spoke to this wheel.	Kan De skaffe en ny Ege til dette Hjuul?	Kahnn Dee skahffă en ny (y like the French u) Ehgă till dennă Yuhl?
Spoon.	Bring a tablespoon — tea-spoon.	Bring en Spiseske — The-ske.	Bring en Speesă-sheh—Teh-sheh.
Spring.	Can you get this spring men-ded?	Kan De faa denne Fjaeder istandsat?	Kahnn Dee foh dennă F'yehr ee-stahnnsaht?
Stages.	Can you not drive two sta-ges?	Kan Du ikke kjøre to Skif-ter?	Kahnn duh ikkă k'yŏ̆ră toh Shift-urr?
Station.	How far is it to the next station?	Hvor langt er det til næste Skifte?	Vohr lahnngt ehr deh till nesstă Shift-ă?
	What is the name of this station?	Hvorledes hedder dette Skifte?	Vohrlchduss hed-durr dettă Shift-ă?
Stockings.	Will you get these stockings washed — mended.	Vær saa snild at faa disse Strømper vaskede — stop-pede.	Vehr soh snill aht foh dissa Strŏ̆mp-urr (the ø like the French en) stoppădă.
	How long before they will be ready?	Naar kan de blive færdige?	Nohr kahnn dee bleevă fehr-diggă?

	English	Dansk	Pronunciation
Strap.	Where can I get a strap?	Hvor kan jeg faa en Rem?	Vohr kahnn yei foh en Rem?
Strawberries.	Have you any strawberries and cream?	Har De Jordbær og Fløde?	Hahrr Dee Yohr-behr ohg Flødĭ?
Sugar.	Bring some loaf — brown sugar.	Bring lidt Raffinade — Puddersukker.	Bring litt Rahlf-ee-nahdă — Pooddurr-sookk-urr.
Supper.	What can I have for supper?,	Hvad kan jeg faa til Aftens?	Vah kahmm yei foh till Ahff-tunns?
Tablecloth.	Have you a clean tablecloth?	Har De en reen Borddug?	Hahr Dee en rehn Bohrd-duhg?
Tarpauling.	Have you a tarpauling that you can put over my baggage?	Har De en Presening at lægge over mit Tøi?	Hahrr Dee en Press-enning ahtt leggă poh mit Tø-ei (ø like the French eu; Tø-ei pronounced in one syllable).
Tea.	Let us have tea at — o' clock.	Lad os faa en Kop stærk The med Kavringer Klokken —	Lah oss foh en Kopp stchrk Teh med Kahv-ringurr Klokkunn —
Telescope.	Can you lend me a telescope?	Kan De laane mig en Kikkert?	Kahnn Dee lohnă mei en Kikkurt?
Thanks.	Thank you.	Tak — Tak skal De have.	Tahkk — Tahkk skahll Dee hah.
Thread.	See Needle.		
Towel.	Please to give me a towel — a clean towel.	Vær saa snild at give mig et Haandtørklæde, et rent Haandtørklæde.	Vehr soh snill ahtt gee (g hard) mei et Hondturrkleh-dä, et rehnt Hondturkleh-dä.
Tub.	Let me have a large tub of cold water in my bedroom.	Lad mig faa en stor Balje koldt Vand i mit Sovekammer.	Lah mei foh en stohr Bahll'yă kollt Vahnn ee mit Sohvă-kahmn-urr.
Tumbler.	See Glass.		

Umbrella.	Can you lend me an umbrella.	Kan De laane mig en Paraply (Regnhat).	Kahnn Dee lohnä mei en Paraply (like the French parapluie).
Veal.	Can I have roast veal — a veal cutlet for breakfast — dinner — supper.	Kan jeg faa Kalvesteg — en Kalve-Cotelet til Frokost — til Middag — til Aftens?	Kahnn yei fok Kahllvä-stehg, en Kahllvä-Kotälet till Frohkost — till Middahg — till Ahfftunns.
Vegetables.	What vegetables have you?	Hvilke Grønsager har De?	Vilkä Grunn-sahg-urr hahrr Dee?
Veil.	Have you a veil?	Har De et Slør?	Hahrr Dee et Slør?
Venison.	Have you any reindeer venison?	Har De Dyresteg?	Hahrr Dee Dyrästehg (y pron. like the French u).
Vinegar.	Bring some vinegar.	Bring lidt Eddikke.	Bring litt Eddikkä.
Wake.	Wake me at — o'clock.	Væk mig Klokken —	Vekk mei Klok-kunn.
Walking-stick.	Can you lend me a walking-stick?	Kan De laane mig en Spadserstok?	Kahnn Dee lohnä mei en Spahsehr-stok?
Washhand-basin.	Bring a washhand-basin.	Bring et Vaskevandsfad.	Bring et Vahss-kä-vahnns-fahd.
Washer-woman.	See Laundress.		
Water,	Let me have a glass — jug of cold — hot — boiling water.	Lad mig faa et Glas — Mugge (Krukke) Vand.	Lah mei foh et Glahss — Moogg̈ä Krookkä Vahnn (the oo in moogg̈ä and in krookkä pron. as in crook).
Watercloset	See Privy.		
Waterfall.	Is there any waterfall near here.	Er der nogen Fos i Omegnen?	Ehr dehr nohg-unn Foss ee Omm-ein-unn?
Way.	See Road.		
What.	What is this?	Hvad er dette — det?	Vahd ehr dettä — deh?

English	Danish	Pronunciation
Wheaten Bread.	See Bread.	
Wheel.	See Grease.	
Wheel-wright. Is there a wheelwright near here?	Boer der en Hjuulmager i Narheden?	Boh-urr dehr en Yuhl-mahg-urr ee Nehr-heddum?
Whip. Have you a whip?	Har De en Svøbe — Pidsk?	Hahrr Dee en Svøbä — Pisk?
Wine. What kinds of wine have you?	Hvilke Sorter Viin har De?	Vilkä Sohrt-urr Veen hahrr Dee?
Bring a glass — bottle of — wine.	Lad mig faa et Glas — en Flaske — Viin.	Lah mei foh et Glahss — en Flahss-kä — Veen.
Bring another bottle of wine.	Skaf mig (me) — os (us) en Flaske Viin til.	Skahff mei — os en Flahskä Veen till.
Wood. Bring some more wood.	Skaf mig — os lidt Ved — Brande.	Skahff mei — os litt Veh — Bren-dä.

Days of the Week.

English	Danish	Pronunciation
Sunday.	Søndag.	Sunn-dahgg.
Monday.	Mandag.	Mahnn-dahgg.
Tuesday.	Tirsdag.	Teers-dahgg.
Wednesday.	Onsdag.	Ohns-dahgg.
Thursday.	Thorsdag.	Thors-dahgg.
Friday.	Fredag.	Freh-dahgg.
Saturday.	Løverdag.	Lurr-dahgg.

Days of the Month.

English	Danish	Pronunciation
January.	Januar	Yahnn-uh-arr.
February.	Februar	Feb-ruh-ahrr.
March	Marts	Mahrrs.
April.	April	Ahprill.
May.	Mai	Mah-ci (pron. in one syllable).
June.	Juni	Yuh-nee.
July.	Juli	Yuh-lee.
August.	August	Ow-goost (ow as in prow, oo as in crook).
September.	September	Sep-tem-burr.
October.	Oktober	Ok-toh-burr.
November.	November	Noh-vem-burr.
December.	December	Dä-sem-burr.

Cardinal Numbers.

One.	Ehn.	Sixteen.	Seist-unn.
Two.	To.	Seventeen.	Sylt-unn.
Three.	Treh.	Eighteen.	Ahtt-unn.
Four.	Feer-ă.	Nineteen.	Nitt-unn.
Five.	Fem.	Twenty.	Tyv-ă.
Six.	Sex.	Thirty.	Tred-ă-vă.
Seven.	Syv.	Forty.	Furră-tyvă.
Eight.	Oïtă.	Fifty.	Femtee.
Nine.	Nee.	Sixty.	Sextee.
Ten.	Tee.	Seventy.	Syltee.
Eleven.	El-ă-vă.	Eighty.	Oïtee.
Twelve.	Toll.	Ninety.	Nittee.
Thirteen.	Trett-unn.	A Hundred.	Et Hoondrădă. (the oo as the book).
Fourteen	Fjohrt-unn.	A Thousand	Et Tuhs-unn.
Fifteen	Feml-unn.	A Million.	En Mill-ee-ohn.

Ordinal Numbers.

First.	Furrstă.	Fourteenth.	Fjohrt-unndă. (the j like the English y).
Second.	Ahnndunn.	Fifteenth.	Femt-unndă.
Third.	Tred-ja. (j like the English y).	Sixteenth.	Seist-unndă.
Fourth.	Fjehrdă.	Seventeenth	Sylt-unndă.
	(see above)	Eighteenth.	Ahtt-unndă.
Fifth.	Femtă.	Nineteenth.	Nitt-unndă.
Sixth.	Sjettă.	Twentieth.	Tyv-unndă.
	(j like the English y).	Thirtieth.	Tred-uvtă.
Seventh.	Syv-unndă.	Fortieth.	Furrgă-tyvunndă.
Eighth.	Ott-unndă.	Fiftieth.	Femtee-unndă.
Ninth.	Nee-unndă.	Sixtieth.	Sextee-unndă.
Tenth.	Tee-unndă.	Seventieth.	Syltee-unndă.
Eleventh.	El-ev-tă.	Eightieth.	Oïtee-unndă.
Twelfth.	Toltă.	Ninetieth.	Nittee-unndă.
Thirteenth.	Trett-unndă.	Hundredth.	Hoon-drădă. (the oo as in book).

APPENDIX.

English.	Norwegian.	Pronunciation.
Ashore. Go ashore.	Gaa i Land.	Goh ee Lahnnd.
Bed. Is my bed made?	Er min Seng redet?	Ehr minn Seng rehd–utt?
Berth. Can I have this berth.	Kan jeg faa denne Køie?	Kahnn yei foh dennä Kø–ei (one syllable).
Bill. Give me the bill.	Lad mig faa Regningen.	Lah mei foh Rei–ning–unn.
The bill is reasonable.	Regningen er ganske billig.	Rei–ning–unn ehr gansk–ä billig.
Boat. The bill is too much.	Regningen er for høi.	Rei–ning–unn ehr fohr hø–ei.
Is there no boat here?	Findes ingen Baad her?	Finnuss ing–unn Bohd hehr?
Let the boat drop down.	Lad Baaden slippe ned.	Lah Bohd–unn slippä nehd.
Can you procure me a boat with a couple of rowers?	Kan man skaffe mig Baad med et Par Roerskarle?	Kahnn mahnn skahffä mei Bohd meh ett Pahrr Rohrs–kahrlä?
Breakfast. I wish to breakfast.	Jeg ønsker at spise Frokost.	Yei ønsk–urr ahtt speesä Frohkosst.
Called. What is that called?	Hvad kaldes dette?	Vahd kahllduss dettä?
Change. Where do we change horses?	Hvor skifter man Heste?	Vohr shift–urr mahnn Hest–ä?
Clean. Clean my boots.	Børst mine Støvler.	Børst meenä Stuvvlurr.
Come. Come in.	Kom ind.	Komm inn.
Conveyance. What conveyance can I have to . . . ?	Hvad Slags Befordring kan jeg faa til?	Vahd Slahgss Befordring kahnn yei foh til?
Cost. What does this cost?	Hvad koster dette?	Vah kost–urr dettä?
Cup. Let me have a cup of coffee.	Lad mig faa en Kop Kaffe.	Lad mei foh en Kopp Kahffä.
Dear. It is very dear.	Det er meget dyrt.	Deh ehr megh–utt dyrt.

Depend.	Can I depend on getting fresh horses on the road?	Kan jeg gjøre Regning paa overalt at faa friske Heste?	Kahnn yei yørä Rei-ning poh overahllt ahtt. foh friskä Hestä?
Dirty.	Send the dirty clothes to the washerwoman.	Send det smudsede Tøi til Vaskekonen.	Send deh smuss-ädä Tø-ei till Vahss-kä-kohn-unn.
Don't.	Don't touch!	Rør ikke!	Rør ikkä!
Eat.	Can I get anything to eat?	Kan jeg faa noget at spise?	Kahnn yei foh Nohg-utt ahtt speesä?
Evening.	In the evening I shall be at home.	Om Aftenen er jeg hjemme.	Omn Ahftt-un-unn ehr yei yemmä.
Expect.	Shall I expect you then?	Kan jeg da vente Dem?	Kahnn yei dah ventä Dem?
Ferry.	Is there a ferry?	Er der en Farge.	Ehr dehr enn Fehrgä?
Fetch.	Fetch me some wine — bread and cheese — butter — milk -- cream — sugar — salt — mustard — pepper — vinegar.	Hent mig Vin — Brød og Ost — Smør — Melk — Fløde — Sukker — Salt — Sennep — Peber — Eddike.	Hent mei Veen — Brød ohg Ohst — Snør — Melk — Flødä — Sookkurr (oo as in erook). Sahllt — Sennep — Pehb-urr — Eddikkä.
Go.	Go away!	Gaa bort or væk!	Goh bohrrt — vekk!
Good-bye!	Good-bye!	Farvel! Adieu!	Fahrrvel! Adyø!
Grease.	Grease the wheels.	Sæt Smörelse til Hjulene.	Sett Snør-ullsä till Juhl-unnä.
Horse.	Horse — immediately.	Hest — strax.	Hest — strahxx.
	Put the horse to.	Spænd for.	Spend fohr.
	How much must I pay for each horse?	Hvormeget maa jeg betale for hver Hest?	Vohr-mehg-utt moh jeg be-tahlä fohr vehr Hest?
Horseback.	I shall perform the journey on horseback. Change horses. See „Change".	Jeg vil gjøre Reisen tilhests.	Yei vil yøra Reis-unn til-hests.
Hungry.	I am hungry -- thirsty.	Jeg er sulten — tørstig.	Yei ehr sult-unn — tørst-igg.

How much.	How much do I — we owe you?	Hvormeget er jeg — ere vi Den skyldig?	Vohr meg–utt ehr yei — chrä vee Dem skyldig?
Inn.	Are there any good inns upon the road?	Findes gode Gjæstgiverste- der paa Veien?	Finnuss gohdä Yeslgeev–urr– stehd–urr poh Vei–unn?
Let.	Let go!	Slip!	Slip!
Light.	Light a fire in the stove.	Læg i Kakkelovnen.	Lægg i Kahkkel–ov v–nunn.
Like.	What would you like to have?	Hvad behager De?	Vah behagg–urr Dee?
Luggage.	I have but little luggage.	Jeg har kun ubetydeligt Tøi.	Yei uahrr koon (oo as in book) uhbä–ty–dä–liggt Tø– ei (one syllable).
Meat.	What kind of meat is there?	Hvad Slags Kjød er der?	Vah Slahggs K'yød ehr dehr?
Meet.	Shall we meet to-night then?	Sees vi saa iaften?	Seh–uss vee soh i–ahfft–unn?
Money.	Here is your money?	Her ere Pengene.	Hehr ehrä Peng–unnä.
Morning.	Good morning — evening!	God Morgen — Aften!	Goh Mor–ning — Ahfft–unn!
Passage.	How much must we pay for the passage?	Hvad koster Billetten?	Vah koss–turr Billett–unn?
Pay.	What have we to pay?	Hvad have vi at betale?	Vah hahvä vee aht betahlä?
Place.	How much does a place in the vessel cost?	Hvor meget koster en Plads paa Skibet?	Vohr mehg–utt koss–tur enn Plahss poh Sheeb–utt?
Plate.	Give me a plate, please.	Vær saa snild at give mig en Tallerken.	Vehr soh snill aht geevä mei enn Tahll–ehr–kunn.
Ready.	Are our rooms ready?	Ere vore Værelser istand?	Ehrä vohrä Vehr–ullsä ee– stahnnd?
River.	Put me over the river.	Sæt mig over Elven.	Sett mei ohvurr Elv–unn.
Road.	Is the road good — bad?	Er Veien god — daarlig?	Ehr Vei–unn gohd–dohrligg?
Room.	Is there no room?	Findes ingen Plads?	Fin–nuss ingunn Plass?
Say.	What did you say?	Hvad sagde De?	Vah sahgg–dä Dee?
Seat.	Be so kind as to take a seat.	Vær saa artig at tage Plads.	Vehr soh ahrtigg ahtt tah Plahss.

	English	Norwegian	Pronunciation
See.	When shall I see you?	Naar faar jeg see Dem?	Nohr fohr yei seh Dem?
Sit.	Sit down a moment.	Sid ned et Øieblik.	Sidd nehd ett O–ei–äblikk.
Shut.	Shut the door.	Luk Døren.	Look (oo as in look) Dør–unn.
Sleep.	Can I sleep here to-night?	Kan jeg faa ligge her inat?	Kahnn yei foh liggĭ hehr eenaht?
Speak.	Do you speak English — Norwegian?	Taler De Engelsk — Norsk?	Tahll–ur Dee Eng–ullsk — Norrsk?
	I cannot speak Norwegian.	Jeg kan ikke tale Norsk.	Yei kahnn ikkä tahllä Norsk.
	You must speak slowly.	De faar tale langsomt.	Dee fohr tahllä lahnngsomt.
	Can I speak to you a moment.	Kan jeg faa tale med Dem et Øieblik.	Kahnn yei foh tahllä meh Dem ett O–ie–blikk?
Steamer.	I wish to go to . . in the steamer.	Jeg önsker at gaa til . . med Dampen.	Yei ønsk–urr ahlt goh till . . meh Dahmmpunn.
Stand.	Stand still.	Staa stille.	Stoh stillä.
	Don't stand in the way.	Staa ikke i Veien.	Stoh ikkä ee Vei–unn.
Thank.	Thank you.	Tak skal De have (literally, thanks you shall have).	Tahkk skahll Dee hah.
	Many thanks.	Mange Tak.	Mahnng–ä Tahkk.
Thirsty.	I am thirsty — what can I have to drink?	Jeg er tørstig — hvad kan jeg faa at drikke?	Yei ehr tørr–stigg — vah kahnn yei foh ahlt drikkä?
Too much.	That is too much.	Det er formeget.	Deh ehr for mehg–utt.
Towel.	Bring me a towel	Bring min et Haandklæde.	Bring mei ett Hondkleh–dä.
Travel.	Did you ever travel this way before?	Har De nogensinde reist denne Vei før?	Hahrr Dee nohg–unn–sindä reist dennä Vei før?
Wait.	Wait a moment.	Vent et Øieblik.	Vent ett Ø–ei–blikk.
Wake.	Wake me early to-morrow.	Væk mig tidlig imorgen.	Vekk mei teed-ligg ee–imorrg-unn.
Want.	What do you want?	Hvad ønsker De?	Vah ønsk–urr Dee?
Where.	Where are we now?	Hvor ere vi nu?	Vohr ehrä vee nuh?

www.ingramcontent.com/pod-product-compliance
Lightning Source LLC
Chambersburg PA
CBHW032123080426
42733CB00008B/1031